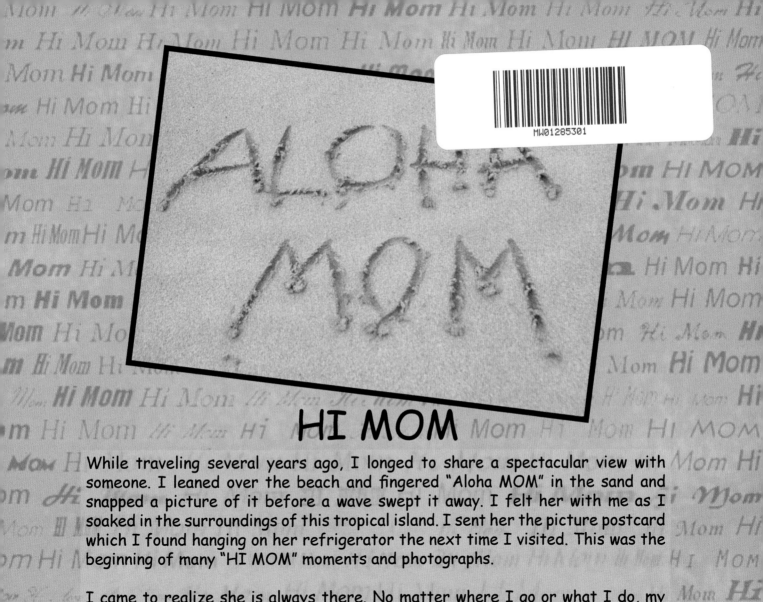

HI MOM

While traveling several years ago, I longed to share a spectacular view with someone. I leaned over the beach and fingered "Aloha MOM" in the sand and snapped a picture of it before a wave swept it away. I felt her with me as I soaked in the surroundings of this tropical island. I sent her the picture postcard which I found hanging on her refrigerator the next time I visited. This was the beginning of many "HI MOM" moments and photographs.

I came to realize she is always there. No matter where I go or what I do, my Mom is always there. She sneaks into my thoughts and provides guidance when I make decisions or to comfort me when things are not going well. I am reminded of her presence by a smell, a taste, or a sound that passes my way and draws me back home to her loving embrace.

May these images remind you of the times you wished your Mom was with you and give you an opportunity to share those thoughts with her.

Throughout the year -

January, February, March,

April, May, June,

This years IOWA State Fair's
Print Shop was visited by:

Hi Mom

The Concrete Beneath You...

July, August,

September, October,

November and December - you are always there!

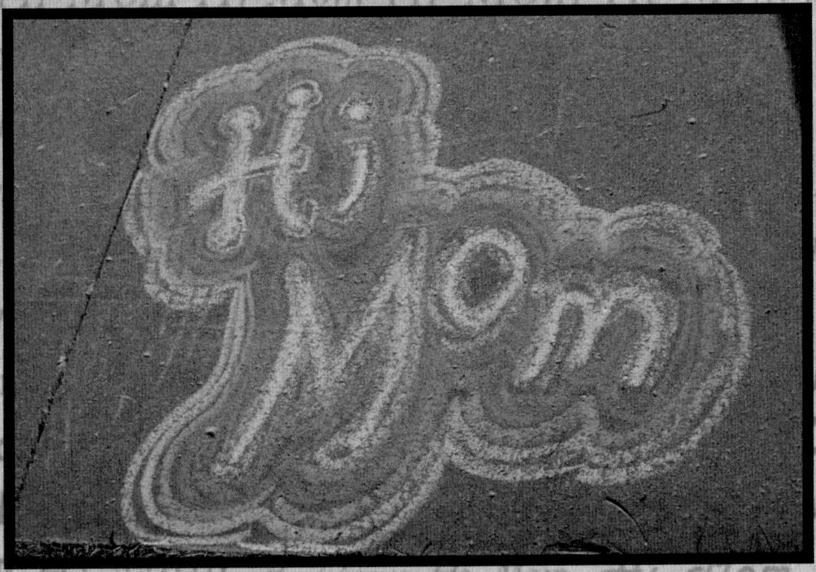

sidewalk chalk

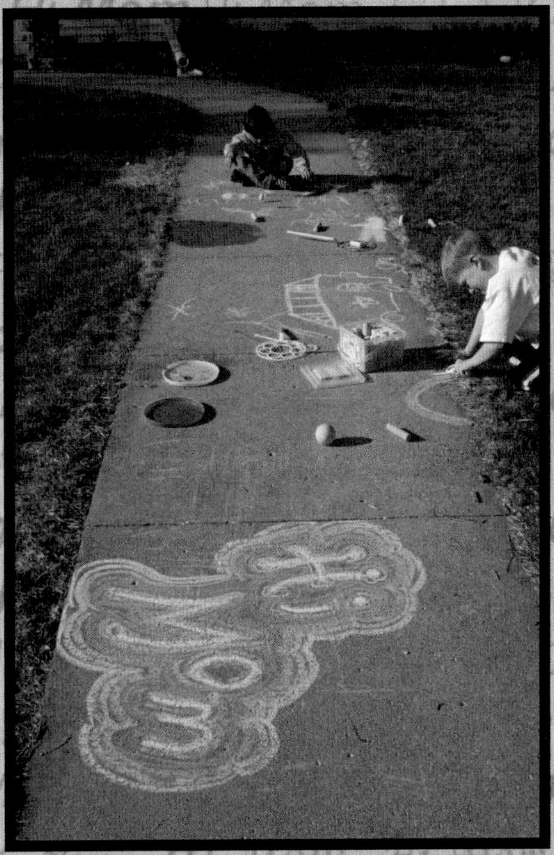

With everything I do....

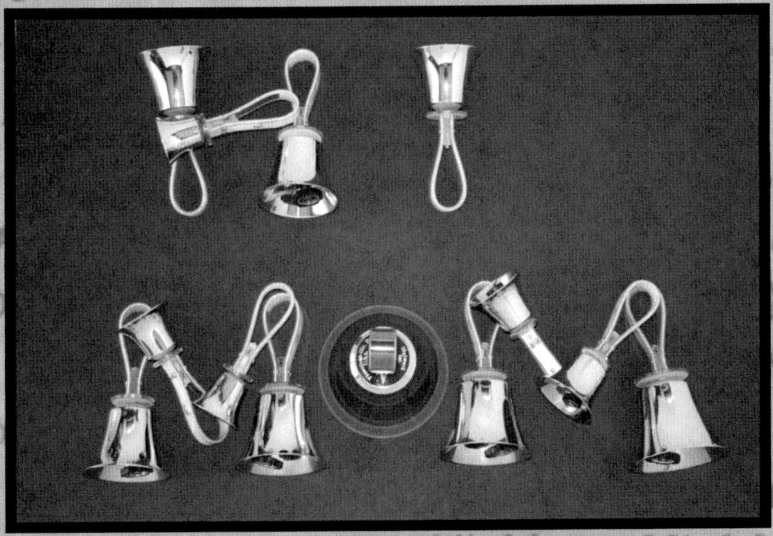

handbells

playing with games and toys

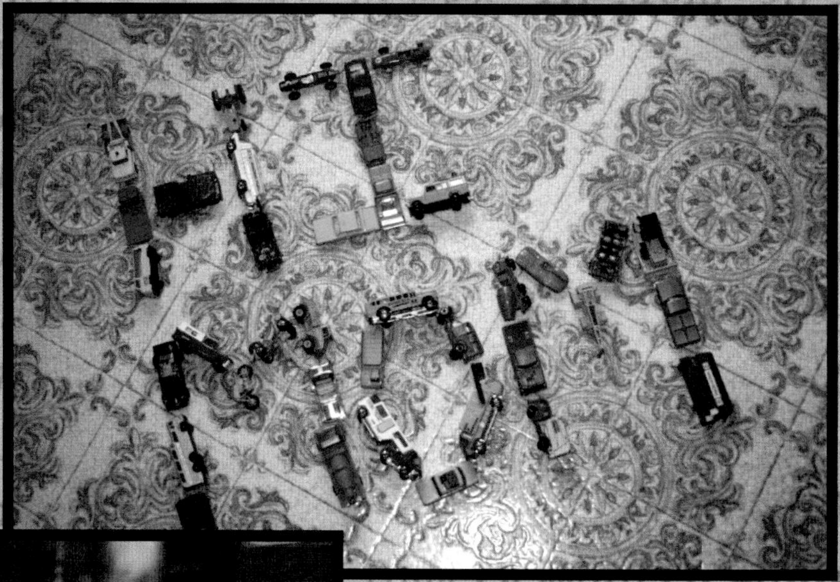

cars

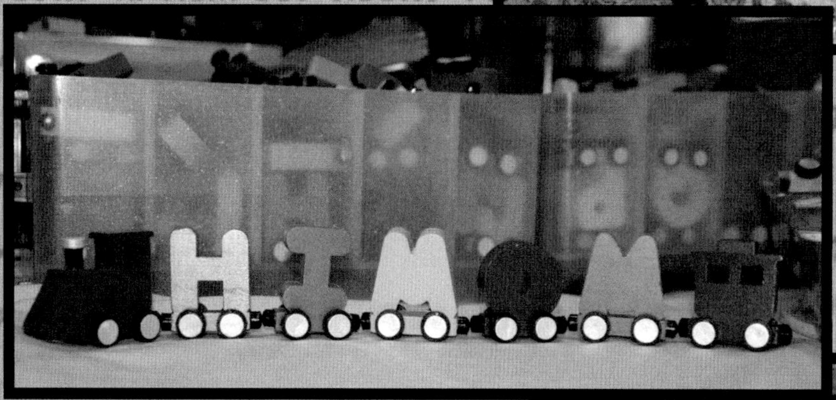

trains

checkers

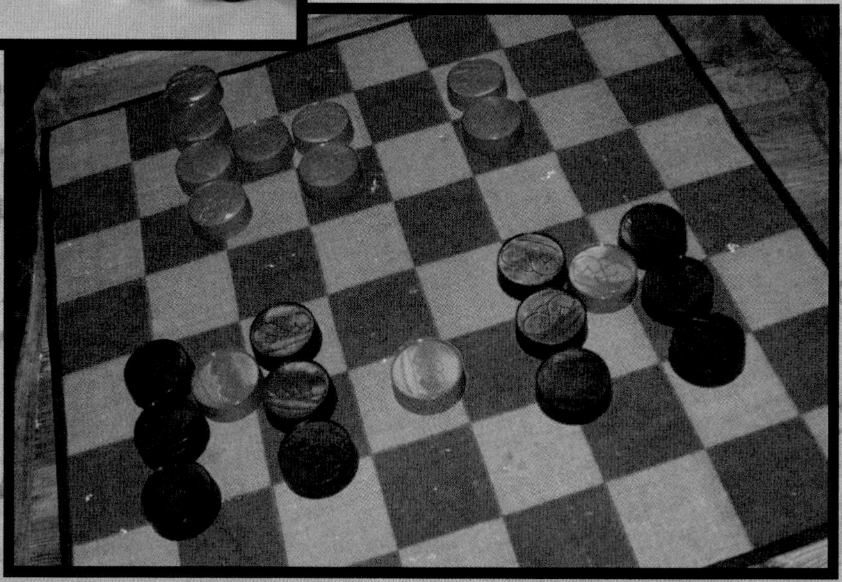

scrabble

dominos

spelling

wood carvings

wood decor

ceramic tiles

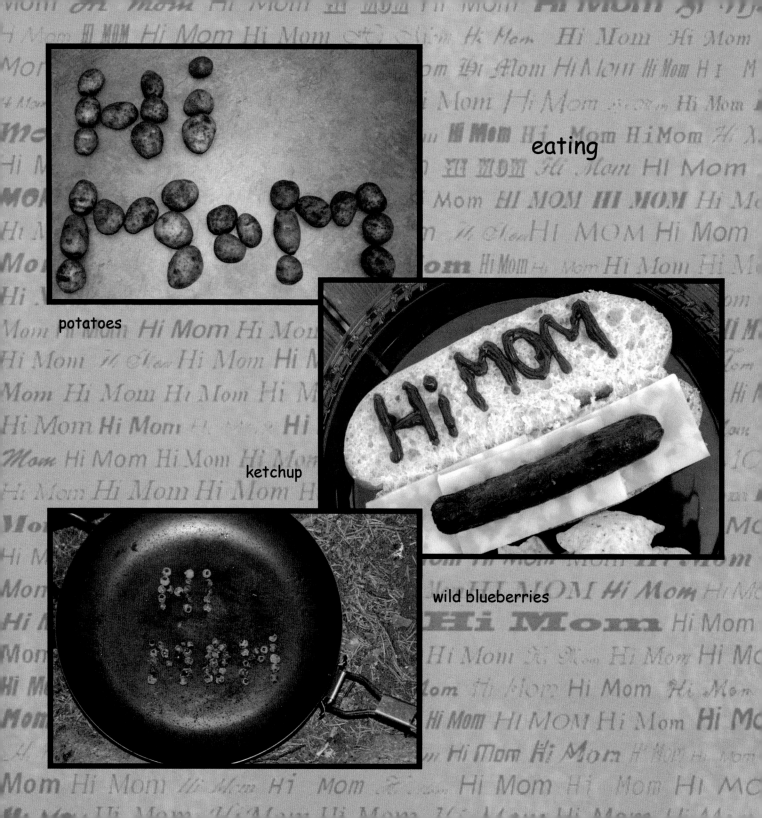

potatoes

eating

ketchup

wild blueberries

spaghetti

apples

crackers

drinking

coffee beans

wine corks

teabags

snacking

candy

popcorn

pecans

jewelry

primping

bobby pins

lipstick

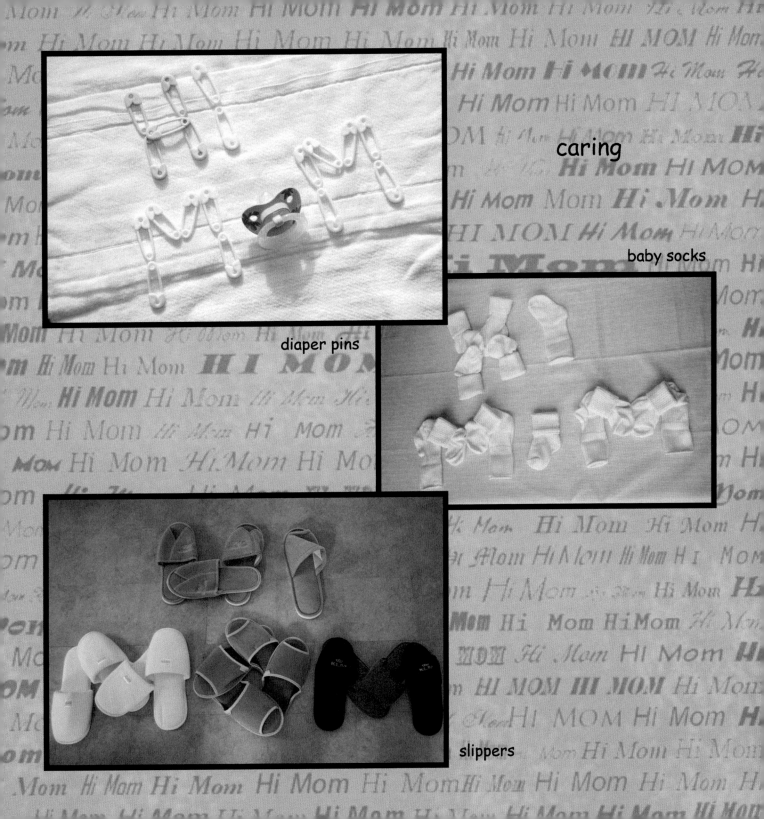

caring

baby socks

diaper pins

slippers

celebrating

painted tattoo

party balloons

cake

ornament

candy canes

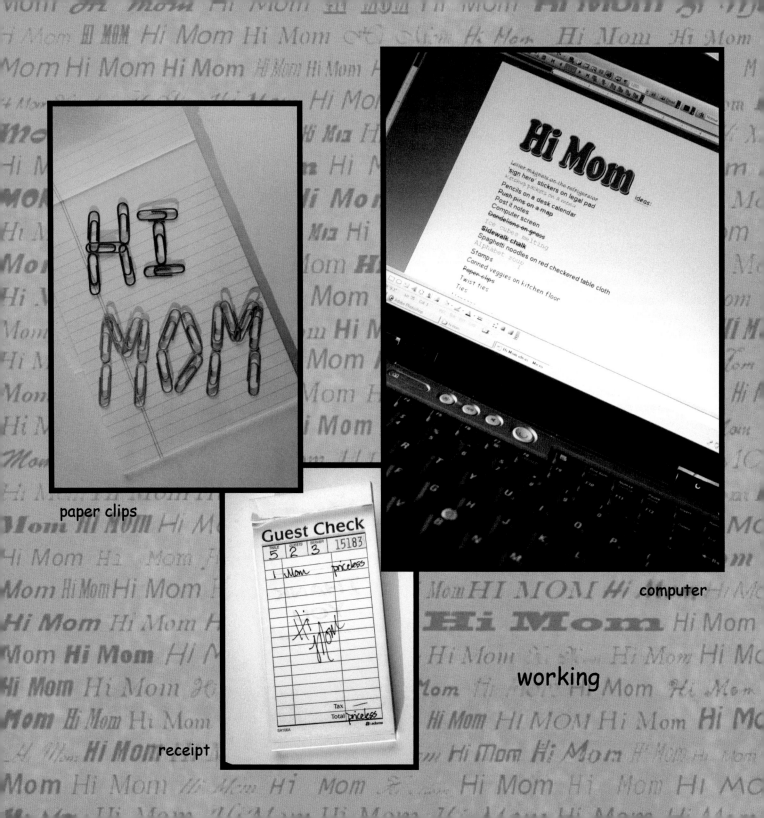

paper clips

computer

working

receipt

touring

Australian art

Korean art

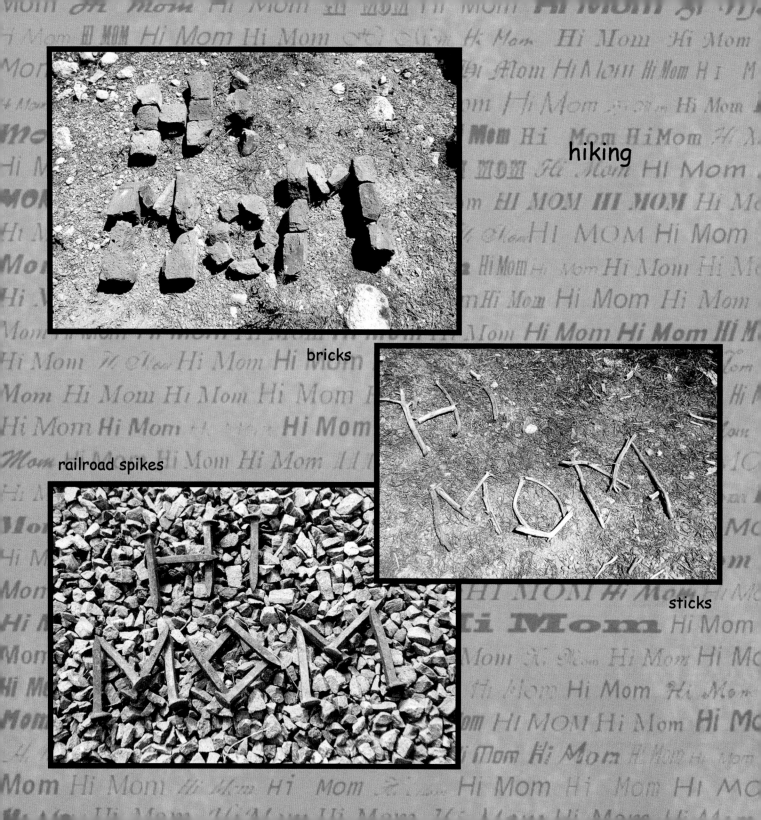

hiking

bricks

railroad spikes

sticks

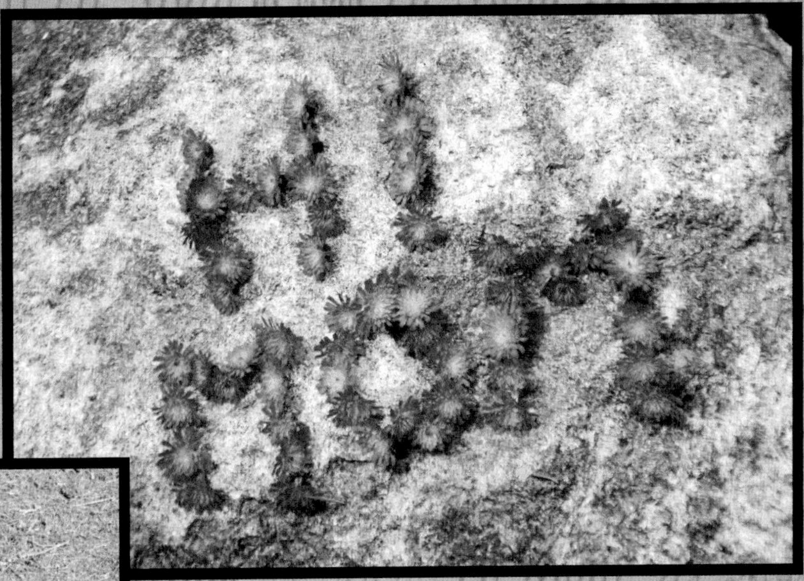

wild flowers

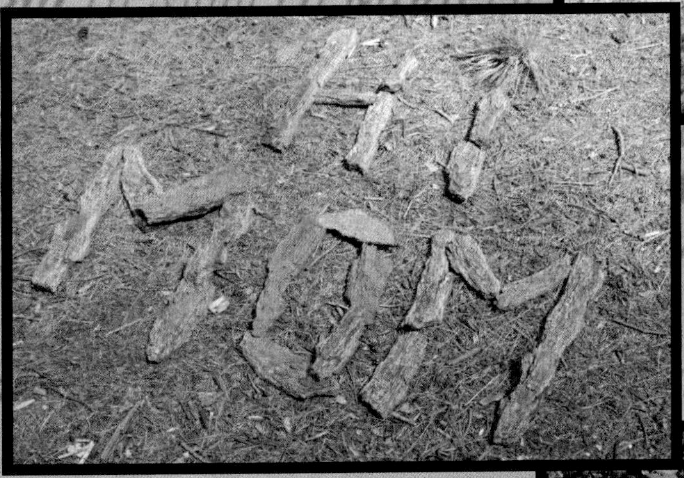

tree bark

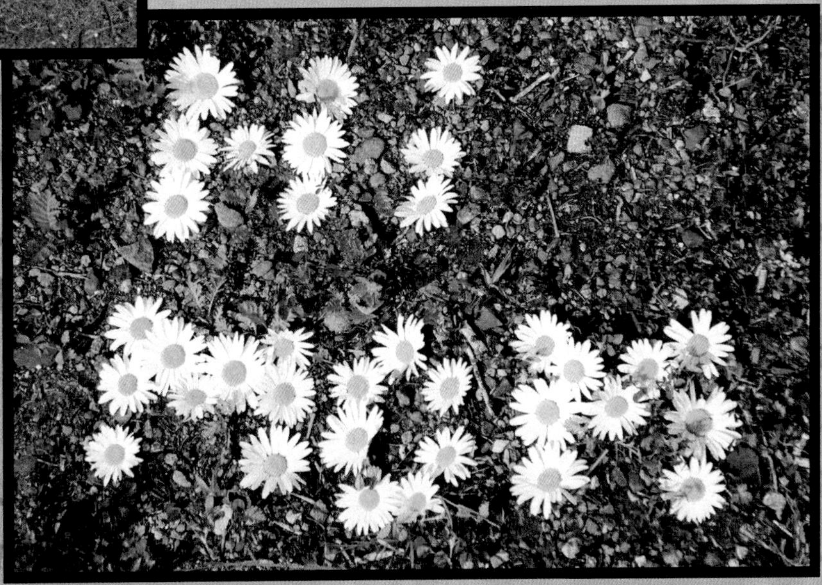

daisies

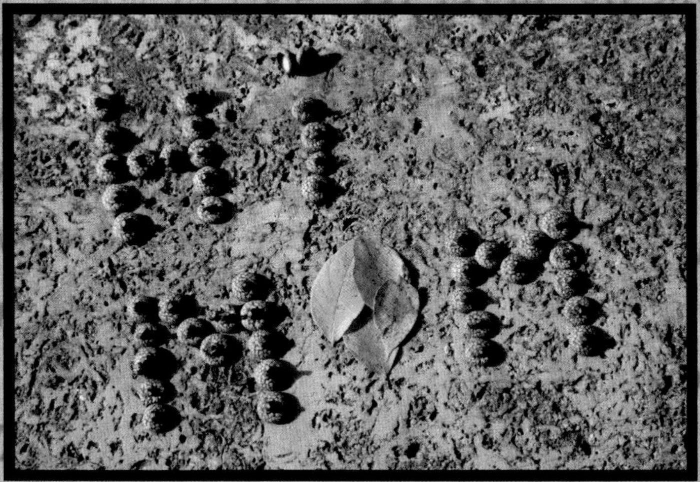

acorn caps

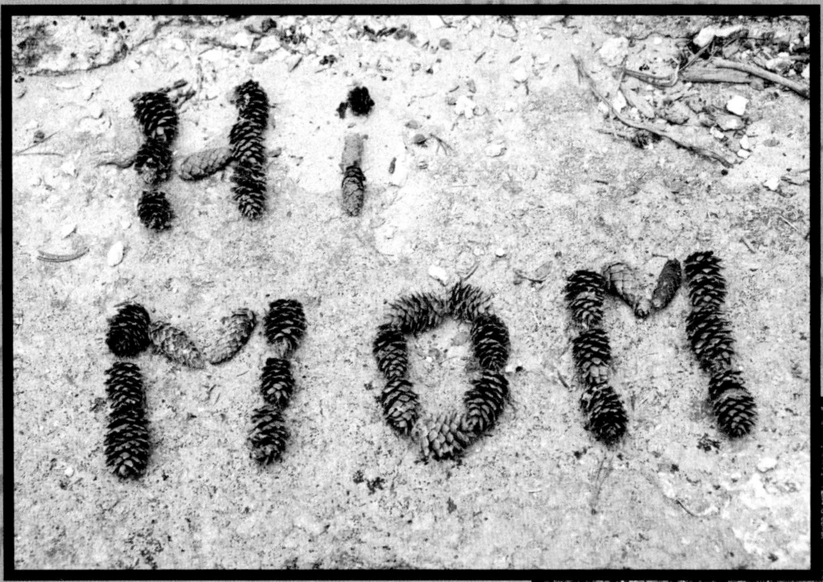

pine cones

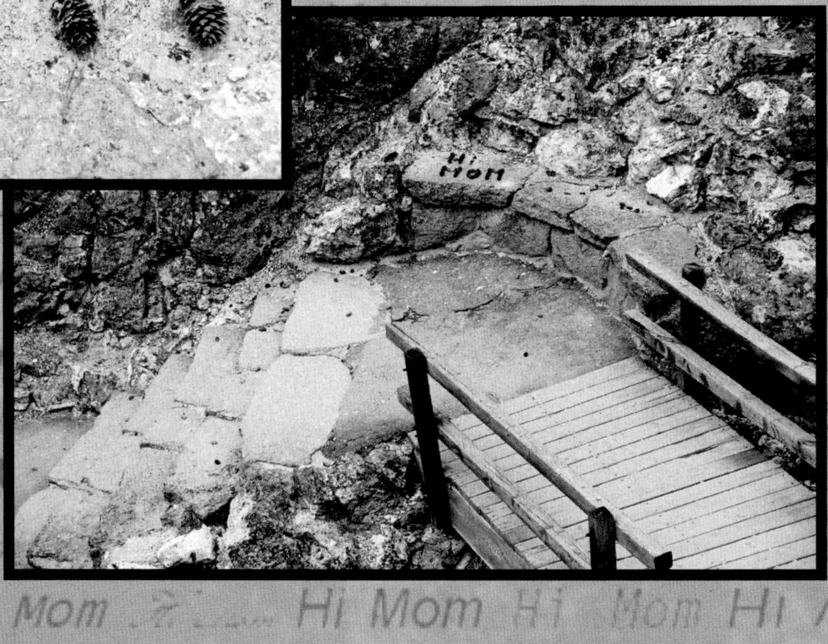

beach combing

sponges

sand

creating

refrigerator
magnets

crayons

buttons

or just having fun you are always there!

smile face buttons

goggle eyes

cups

Hi Mom

Hi Mom

No matter where I go...

IOWA
HI MOM
POLK

your backyard or around the world

Arizona

Alaska

California

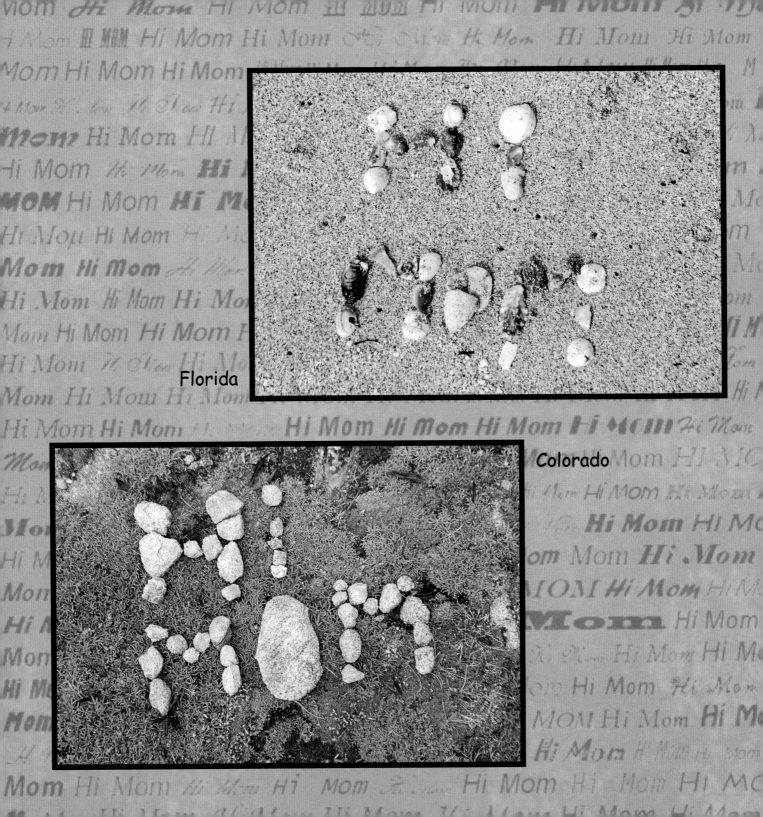

Florida

Colorado

Indiana

Minnesota

Montana

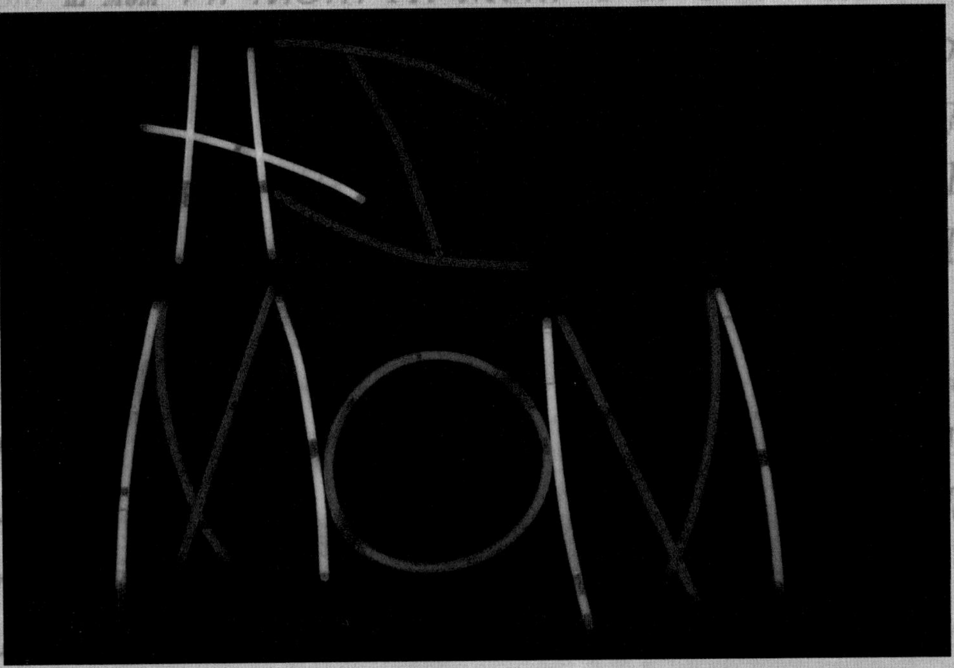

Nevada

Pennsylvania

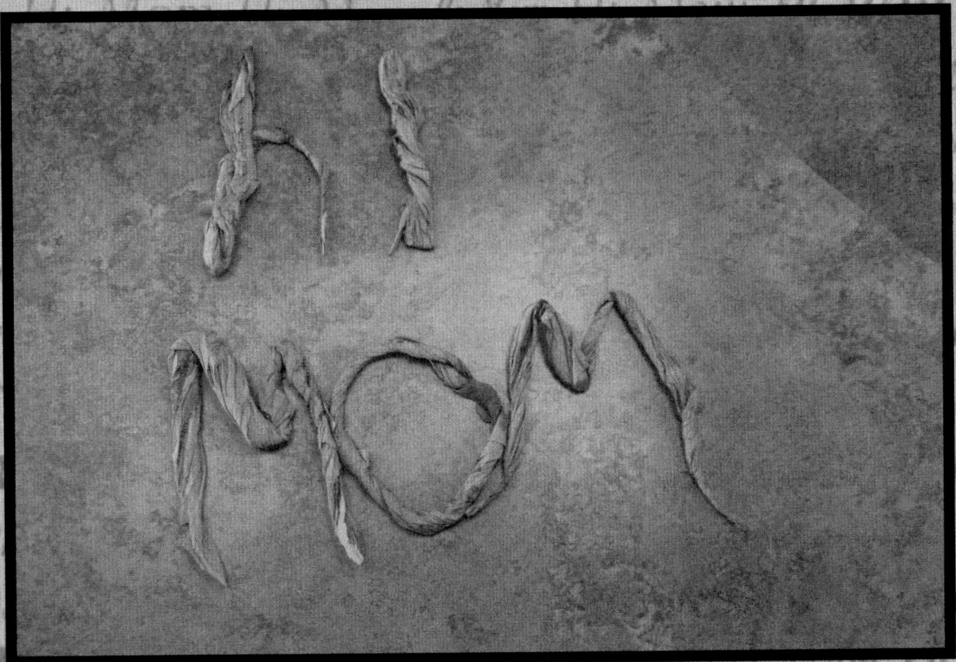

New Jersey

New Mexico

North Dakota

Washington

Wisconsin

Australia

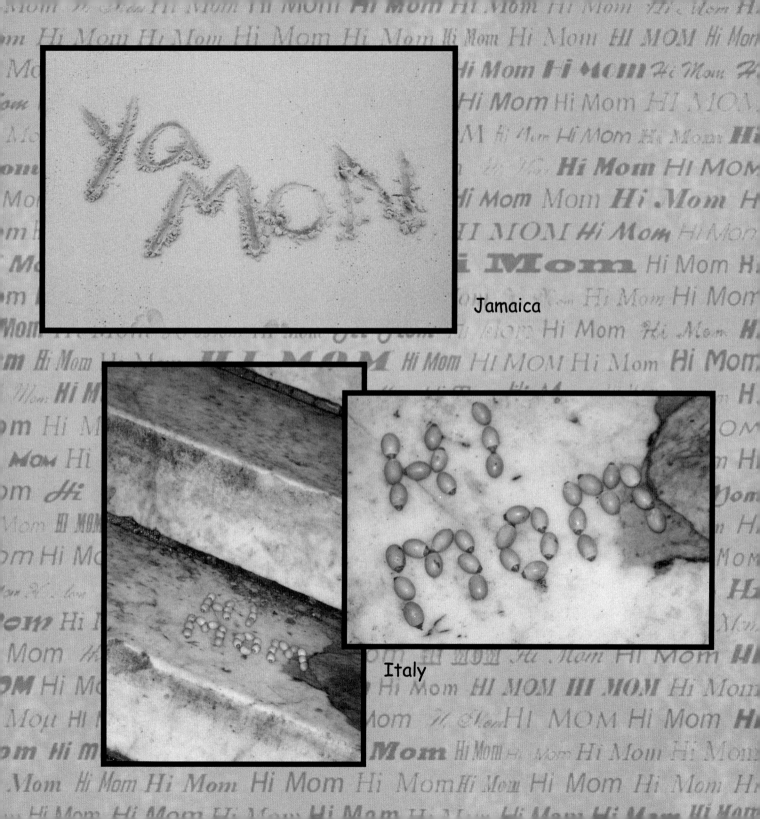

Jamaica

Italy

Spain

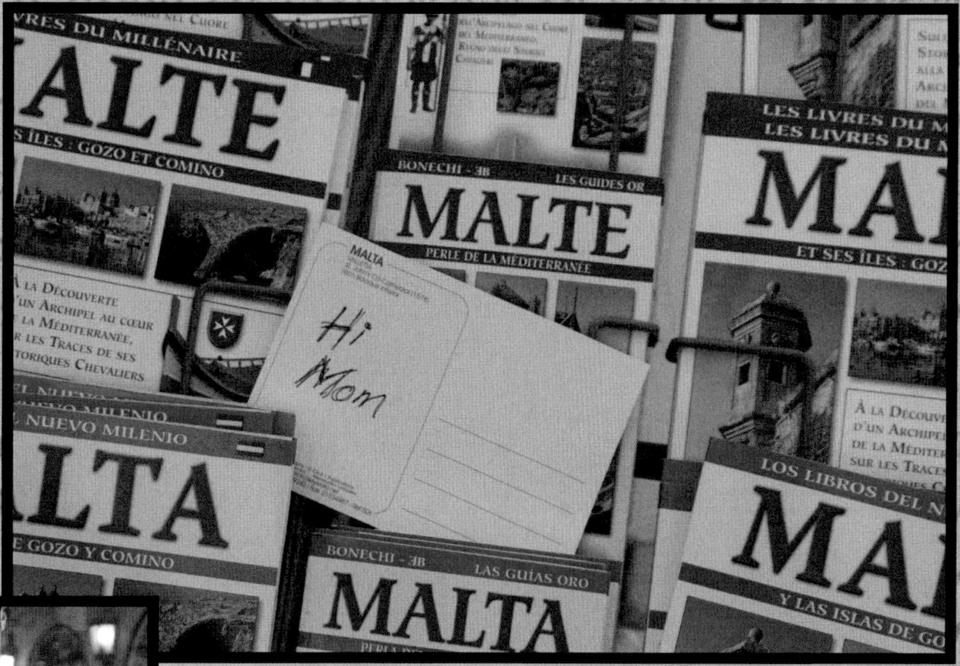

Malta

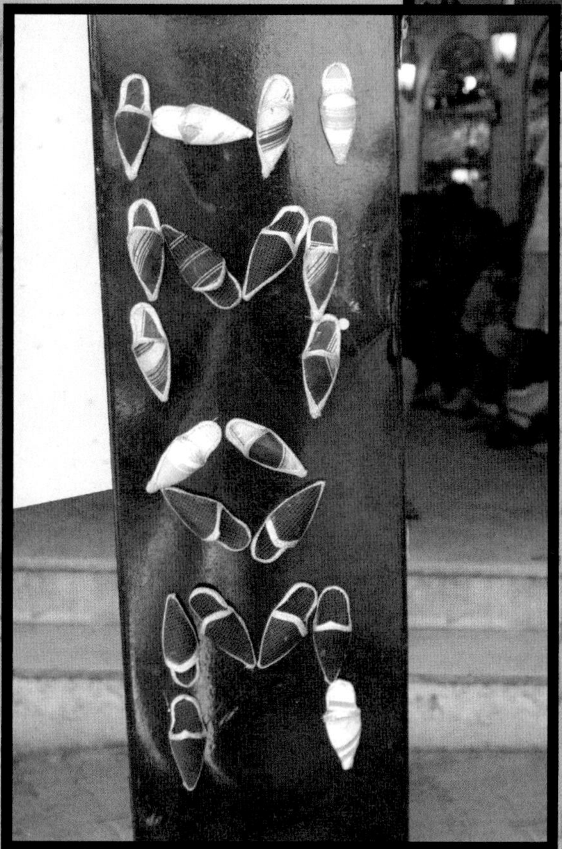

Tunisia

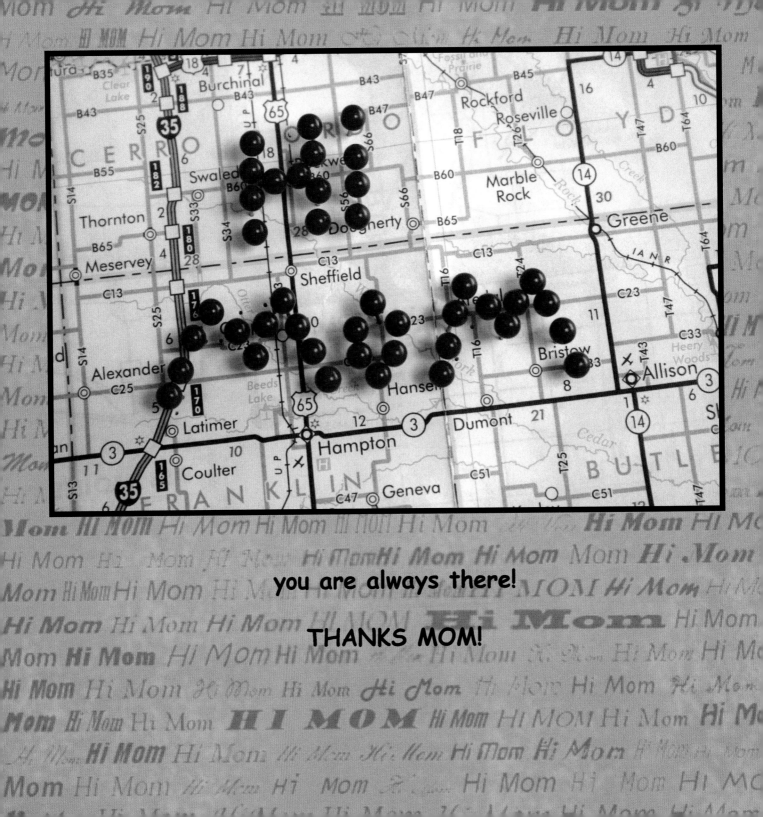

you are always there!

THANKS MOM!

60499586R00027